JEFFY'S LOOKIN' AT ME!

by
Bil Keane

FAWCETT GOLD MEDAL • NEW YORK

A Fawcett Gold Medal Book

Published by Ballantine Books

Copyright © 1973, 1974 by The Register & Tribune Syndicate
Copyright © 1976 by CBS Publications, The Consumer Publishing Division of CBS Inc.

ISBN 0-449-12869-5

Manufactured in the United States of America

First Fawcett Gold Medal Edition: January 1977
First Ballantine Books Edition: June 1983
Third Printing: July 1985

"The little bell means go back and start over again."

"Mr. George is very proud of me. We've had three days of school and I haven't missed ONE DAY so far."

"How old are girls when they turn into 'the opposite sex'?"

"I was afraid you weren't home 'cause I couldn't hear Daddy snoring."

"My flavorite lunch is college cheese."

"Mommy, I've been tryin' to remember. Whose kid
was I when you were a little girl?"

"Why did we all stand over at one side for this
picture that Mommy took?"

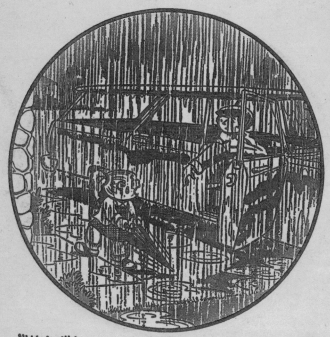

"Wait till I open my umbrella so I won't get all wet!"

"Fish aren't very good pets. They're too hard to hug."

"When I get big will you buy me some kids so I can play Mommy, too?"

"My good ol' beetle was swimmin' around and Dolly
flushed him away!"

"Mommy! PJ just broke up a puzzle I spent half my life doing!"

"First, you'll notice that, contrary to what you may have heard, I do not have horns, two heads or wear a swastika."

"Don't go 'way, Mommy! I need somebody to cry to."

"Scott wants to know if I
want a hamster."

"No, I don't want a ham-
ster."

"When the leaves get rusty, they fall off."

"Daddy, can you fix my football so it doesn't
wobble when I throw it?"

"I can't wear THAT! Billy wore it last year and everybody will remember it!"

"How come, Mommy? I had 49 things when I went to
school today and now there's only 47!"

"I did the whole project myself! My dad is just helpin' me CARRY it!"

"Grandma! Your stockings come in TWO PIECES!"

"That's not funny! Just say 'excuse me' and forget it."

"Coach bet me a dime that I couldn't keep quiet for
five minutes, and know what? I lost."

"Could I have one of the pieces with a handle on it?"

"Daddy went to sleep without saying his prayers."

"I can't get this darn child-proof top off the aspirin."

"That's NOT a lollipop — it's a thermometer."

"But, Mommy! DADDY'S don't get sick!"

"Daddy must REALLY be sick. He doesn't even want to watch TV."

"Aw — How can we help Daddy get better by goin'
outside to play?"

"Do you want me to help hold Daddy down while you
give him his medicine?"

"If Daddy has a baby, I hope it's a girl."

"I'm makin' you a get-well card, Daddy. Can you
show me how to draw a flower?"

"I wish Daddy would hurry up and get better. I'm
tired of TV dinners."

"... and here are the crayons and Dolly went to get you her Peter Rabbit book..."

"Daddy's feelin' a lot better, Mr. Horton, but you can't talk to him right now 'cause he's playing golf."

"It's like Saturday every day havin' Daddy home."

"Daddy's all better — He's dressed in REAL CLOTHES!"

"Mommy! Did you give Daddy a note sayin' why he was absent from work?"

"Darn! The school bus missed me today, Mommy!"

"Has anyone seen my comb?"

"Did Mommy hurt herself?"

"Is it okay to pray before the test if I don't do it out loud?"

"I'm leaving my wallet under the pillow so the tooth fairy can just put the money right in it."

"That's okay, Mommy — we won't tell Daddy."

"I forgot to tell you about the day I threw crayons at
Mary Ann Knazer."

"Why didn't you think of that before I dressed you?"

"Try callin' Santa Claus — that always
works for Mommy!"

"I hope we have an OLD-FASHIONED Christmas,
like we had when I was little."

"Why don't you read the whole poem on the card
instead of just who it's from?"

"I don't have to kiss you 'cause I don't even
BELIEVE in mistletoe!"

"I said 'Merry Christmas' to the mailman, but
he didn't look too happy."

"Mommy, last year Santa's eyes were BLUE and now
they look brown."
"Yes — he got contact lenses!"

"Now it's even beginning to SMELL like Christmas!"

". . .ninety-seven, ninty-eight, ninety-nine, ONE dol-
lar. . .one, two, three, four. . ."

"It's this year's mystery card — Jane and Ed . . .
Jane and Ed WHO?"

"Mommy! It's some trick or treaters — and they're SINGIN'!"

"It's very late — I better get in my manger!"

"It's a Christmas present from God!"

"Mommy! Jeffy's bein' like Scrooge!"

"Why aren't you usin' the shaving cream I bought you
for Christmas?"

"Why did this ball fall off? Is it dead?"

"Gee---the room looks empty."

"Do I HAFTA wear it to school? Everybody'll say, 'Ha, Ha, I know what you got for Christmas!'"

"Daddy always makes the tires look flat."

"It's one of your children, Thel. Says it's important."

"Mommy, Dolly is eating my french fries."

"Open wide."

"Boy, PJ! Don't you have all the flavor sucked out of
your thumb by now?"

"You must eat a lot of peanut butter and jelly Grandma, 'cause you always have plenty of it when we come."

"It's all better now, huh, Mommy?"

"I couldn't help it. He loosed my temper."

"Melanie and Buddy came over here to play 'cause
their mommy is readin' a book."

"Look at the big plane, Jeffy!"
"That's littler than the one I got for Christmas."

"Boy, Mommy, you're so good at takin' care of kids I
bet you could even get a job as a BABY SITTER!"

"The first one who says 'What did you bring us, Grandma?' goes to his room!"

"Wow, Mommy! You look brand new!"

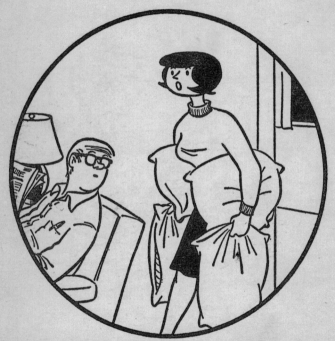

"This should quiet them down. I confiscated their weapons."

"Those are our very best cups. You have to be careful
not to drop 'em."

"Can I help you put diapers on the trash cans, Daddy?"

"Naughty door! You hurt PJ's fingers!
You naughty door!"

"Mommy, what's a dullard?"

"I'll be very careful crossing the street 'cause if a truck ran over me then I'd have to go out and buy angel clothes."

"Will you fix the TV, Mommy? All it does is go 'BEEE-
EEEE-EEEEEEEP!'"

"You don't know HOW to sleep over, Mike. You're not s'posed to sleep — you're just s'posed to TALK."

"Mommy can't come to the phone now, Mrs. Allen.
She's working on the two-times table."

"It doesn't play right now 'cause Barfy was chewing on it."

"Did you 'member to put a ZIP COAT on that letter?"

"I can hardly hear it tick, Daddy — How do you turn
up the volume?"

"At Aunt Kay's we got to sleep in the bump bed! Billy slept in the top bump and I got the bottom bump!"

"This syrup is startin' to be all gone."

"Be brave, Daddy, it'll only sting for a minute —
that's a good soldier . . ."

"We're getting our breakfast but we can't find the ice cream scoop."

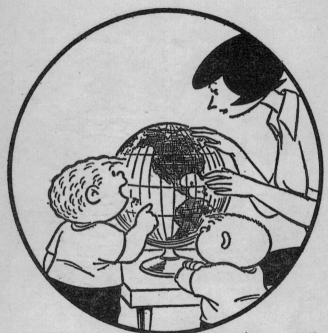

"Where's OUR house, Mommy? Where's OUR house?"

" 'Miss' means you're not married, and 'Missus' means you're married, and 'Miz' means it's a secret."

"Kevin's mom writes her notes to the teacher on pretty blue paper with a PEN and Rocky's mother TYPES hers and . . ."

"Mommy! The teakettle wants you!"

"My teacher found two mistakes in this note you wrote him."

"Quick, Mommy! I need a bang-aid!"

"Mommy! Barfy's not sharing!"

"Wow! Look at that big spider! It's called a GAR-
GANTULA!"

"Mommy, should I hold my fork the right way or the way I do at home?"

"A lot of my friends have neat metal things on their teeth! Can I get some?"

"It'll be okay for school today. Just don't raise your hand."

"You can go to another part of the store, Mommy.
I can watch myself."

"Talk about ROUGH DAYS! Miss Johnson yelled at us
so much her throat got sore and she had to go
home—then I had to run the class."

"Read good and loud, Daddy, so I don't fall asleep."

"Carol's mother and father are gettin' a DI-
VORCE---can we get one of those, too?"

"Little Miss Muffet sat on a tuppet eating her spiders away..."

"Can Dianne's new puppy come into our house? His name is Puddles."

"We learned some new words in art today. The teacher sprayed paint all over his clothes."

"He doesn't even have TRAINING WHEELS!"

"Look! A robin red vest!"

"For Father's Day let's all go in together and get
Daddy a new kite."

"We lost the game again, but the coach bought us a treat anyway."

"Mommy, we lost the sound on this key."

"Can you get some of that three-colored kind? It's
called Napoleon."

"Will the fingernail fairy leave money under my
pillow?"

"Mommy, how long did it take me to grow up?"